BERKLEE PRESS

berklee rock guitar chord
DICTIONARY

rick peckham

Edited by Jonathan Feist

Berklee Press

Vice President: David Kusek
Dean of Continuing Education: Debbie Cavalier
Managing Editor: Jonathan Feist
Chief Operating Officer: Robert F. Green
Senior Designer: Robert Heath
Editorial Assistants: Yousun Choi, Emily Goldstein, Claudia Obser
Cover Designer: Kathy Kikkert

ISBN: 978-0-87639-106-8

1140 Boylston Street
Boston, MA 02215-3693 USA
(617) 747-2146

Visit Berklee Press Online at
www.berkleepress.com

DISTRIBUTED BY

HAL•LEONARD®
CORPORATION
7777 W. BLUEMOUND RD. P.O. BOX 13819
MILWAUKEE, WISCONSIN 53213

Visit Hal Leonard Online at
www.halleonard.com

Contents

Introduction

I've been teaching at Berklee College of Music for over twenty years by now, and it's an amazing place to call my professional home. My responsibilities include teaching private students, administrating for the Guitar Department (with Chair Larry Baione), auditions for the College, and work with online courses for Berkleemusic.com.

In the hundreds of auditions I've done, I'm nearly always able to learn at least one thing from every guitarist I see. The lesson I'm learning from the guitarist can involve a wide range of topics. I may see a new fingering for a common chord shape, an interesting approach to a groove or riff, a performance of a transcription of Guitar Hero previously unknown to me, all the way to an inspiring, humbling "Grand Canyon moment" where I'm seeing a new world class performer on the guitar. I've always found it to be very rewarding.

We all need to know how to play chords. As guitarists, we're all responsible to learn the chordal vocabulary necessary to express ourselves through our own compositions or those of others. There are thousands of chord voicing variations that work well on the guitar. This book is intended as a reference guide for chord shapes used in the rock style.

How to Use This Book

Every voicing appears in standard notation, tablature (TAB), and chord block notation. The fingerings presented here are meant to be practical, and unreasonable stretches have been kept to a minimum.

The "Open Position Chords" section should get you going on the basic chord forms that most guitarists learn first. Fingerings are presented in the chord block graphics, found above the standard notation and TAB staves. If a suggested chord fingering is awkward for you at first, please compare it to the fingering you prefer. If you're getting a full sound, with no muffled tones or errant string bumps, your variation may be the better one for you. You may wish to consider the fingering presented here as an alternate fingering, as it is very common for musical context to dictate an easier, more convenient alternate choice.

The "Capo Transposition Chart" should be useful to guitarists who use capos. The chart shows how each of basic open-position chord shapes can be taken through all keys. The fret position for the capo dictates the root of the chord sound. This is a well-established way for guitarists to take their music into seemingly remote keys, most often to match a comfortable key for the singer of the moment.

Power chords, triadic shapes, barre chords, and other common voicings are given their own sections, allowing you to codify what you already know and expand things into areas perhaps unexplored up until now.

Speaking of unexplored areas, the section "Using Open Tunings" presents you with chord shapes convenient to those using the alternate tunings of "Drop D," "Double-Drop D," and "Open G." These simple reconfigurations of the guitar have seen frequent use, as heard in the music of Neil Young, the Beatles, the Rolling Stones, and the Black Crowes. Where will these new sounds take you and your music?

General Suggestions

"Practice makes perfect" is no match for "Perfect practice makes perfect." Perfect practice involves consistent use of a metronome (or drum loops on a sequencer) and an electronic tuner.

While practicing with a metronome, you're able to experience and interact with perfect, quantized time. The better your groove, the better the metronome will sound! Go for a full sound with a great time feel whenever you're playing guitar.

The widespread availability of electronic tuners has made an amazing difference for guitarists worldwide. Making frequent use of a tuner will allow you to play in tune—and it's never a good time to play out-of-tune! In my online teaching, one of the most frequently noticed problems has to do with the tuning of the guitar. It only takes a moment and it's so easy to do...

When playing new chord shapes on the guitar, be very careful to fret the chords as precisely as possible. Your fretting hand should be very close to the intended fret (without being on top of it). This is the best way to allow the guitar fret to produce the most beautiful, pure sound.

Many of the chord voicings presented in this book contain a string that's supposed to be skipped. Extraneous string sounds interfere with our musical expression in a serious way. Depending on the key of the chord of the moment, these extra strings can cause some disastrous clashes with the desired chord sound. Using the sides of your fretting fingers to mute the unwanted strings and taking care with your strumming can eliminate these problems. Take special care with the details. It makes a huge difference.

The last section, the "Glossary of Common Chord Voicings," provides you with instant access to useable shapes for major, minor, suspended 4, diminished, augmented, dominant 7, dominant 7(9), dominant 7(♯9), dominant 7(♭9), dominant 7♯5, dominant 7 suspended 4, major 7, minor 7, and diminished 7 voicings. The material is sorted into twelve keys, so find the root or bass note of the chord you're looking for, and look through the various chord qualities to find one or more voicings that will work for you.

I sincerely hope that this material will be helpful to you and wish you the best in all of your musical endeavors.

—Rick Peckham

PART I.
CHORD
TYPES

Chapter 1.
Open Position Chords

Major (Roots: CAGED)

C
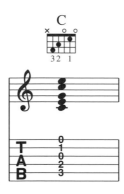

A
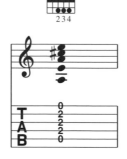

G
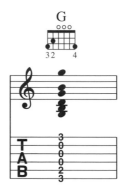

E
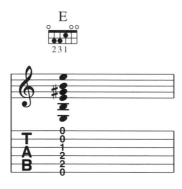

D
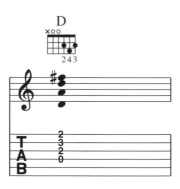

Dominant 7 (Roots: CAGED)

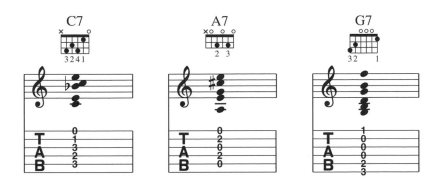

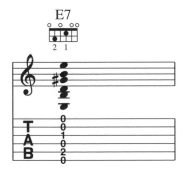

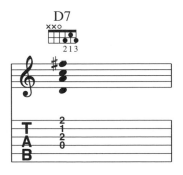

Minor (Roots: AED)

Note: C and G forms are impractical for minor shapes.

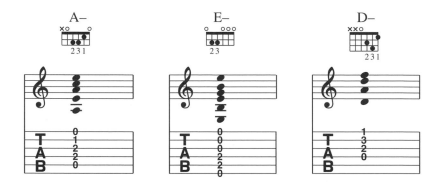

Other Common Chords: F Major, F Minor, B Dominant 7

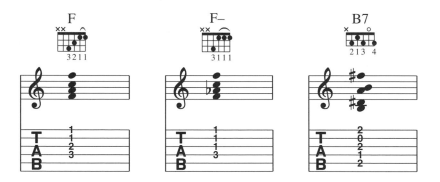

Capo Transposition Chart

Playing open-position chords with a capo on the given fret (designated by a roman numeral) will yield a chord sound that's transposed to the indicated root. For example, a C major chord shape played with the capo on the third fret (III) sounds E♭ major. Capos are commonly used on the first seven frets, so those are the positions listed.

Open chord shape	C	C7	A	A–	A7	G	G7	E	E–	E7	D	D–	D7	F	F–	B7
I	C♯ or D♭	C♯7 or D♭7	A♯ or B♭	A♯– or B♭–	A♯7 or B♭7	G♯ or A♭	G♯7 or A♭7	F	F–	F7	D♯ or E♭	D♯– or E♭–	D♯7 or E♭7	F♯ or G♭	F♯– or G♭–	C7
II	D	D7	B	B–	B7	A	A7	F♯ or G♭	F♯– or G♭–	F♯7 or G♭7	E	E–	E7	G	G–	C♯7 or D♭7
III	D♯ or E♭	D♯7 or E♭7	C	C–	C7	A♯ or B♭	A♯7 or B♭7	G	G–	G7	F	F–	F7	G♯ or A♭	G♯– or A♭–	D7
IV	E	E7	C♯ or D♭	C♯– or D♭–	C♯7 or D♭7	B	B7	G♯ or A♭	G♯– or A♭–	G♯7 or A♭7	F♯ or G♭	F♯– or G♭–	F♯7 or G♭7	A	A–	D♯7 or E♭7
V	F	F7	D	D–	D7	C	C7	A	A–	A7	G	G–	G7	A♯ or B♭	A♯– or B♭–	E7
VI	F♯ or G♭	F♯7 or G♭7	D♯ or E♭	D♯– or E♭–	D♯7 or E♭7	C♯ or D♭	C♯7 or D♭7	A♯ or B♭	A♯– or B♭–	A♯7 or B♭7	G♯ or A♭	G♯– or A♭–	G♯7 or A♭7	B	B–	F7
VII	G	G7	E	E–	E7	D	D7	B	B–	B7	A	A–	A7	C	C–	F♯7 or G♭7

Chapter 2.
Power Chords

Power chords have the root, fifth, and sometimes the octave.

Strings ⑥⑤

Sixth String Root Names for Power Chords with Bass Notes on 6th String

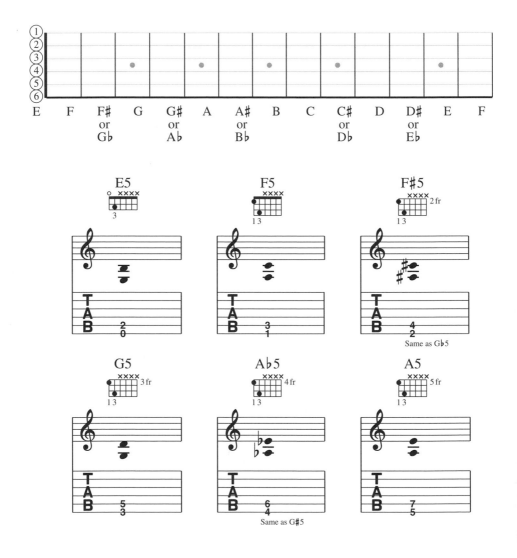

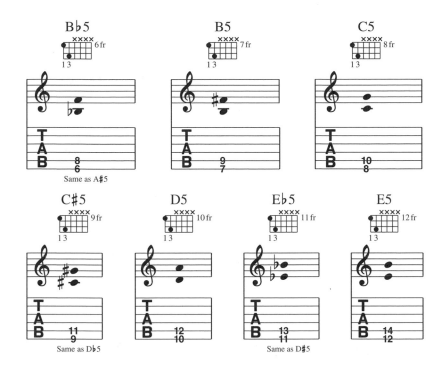

Strings ⑤④

Fifth String Root Names for Power Chords with Bass Notes on 5th String

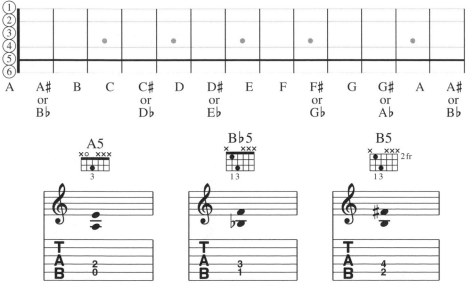

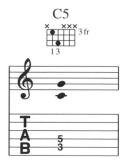

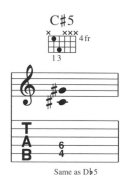

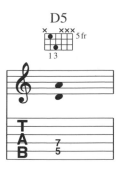

Same as D♭5

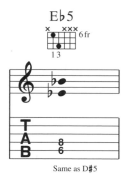

Same as D♯5

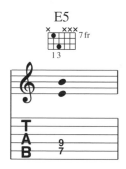

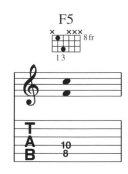

Same as G♭5

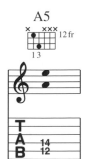

Same as G♯5

Strings ⑥⑤④

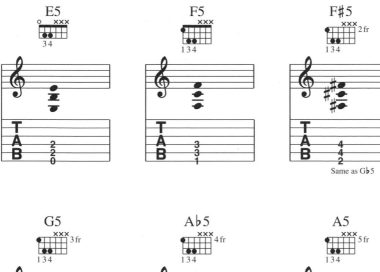

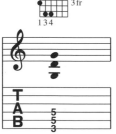

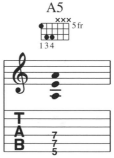

Same as G♭5

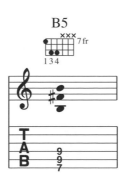

Same as G♯5

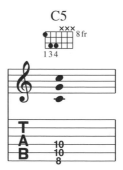

Same as A♯5

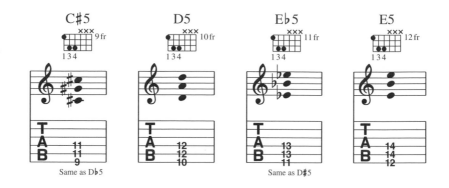

Same as D♭5   Same as D♯5

Strings ⑤④③

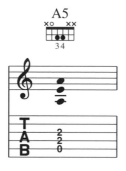

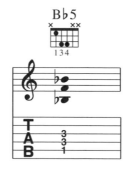

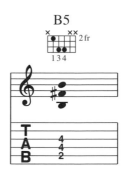

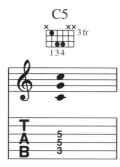

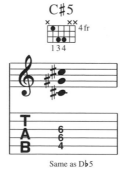

Same as D♭5

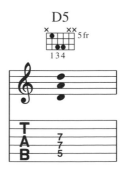

E♭5

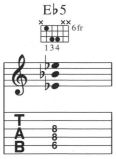

Same as D♯5

E5

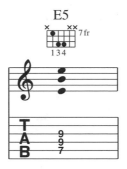

F5

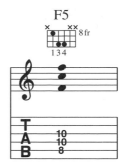

F♯5

Same as G♭5

G5

A♭5

Same as G♯5

A5

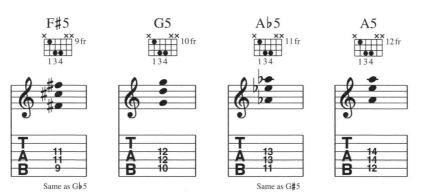

Etude: Power Chords in Twelve Keys

This etude features power chords in twelve keys, using open strings wherever possible.

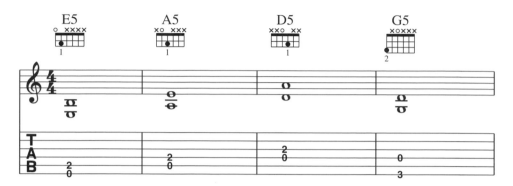

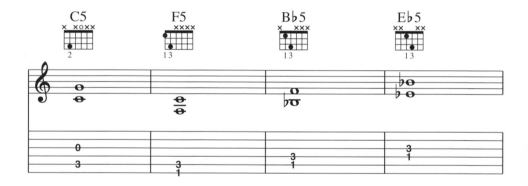

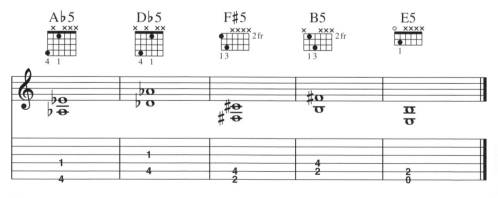

Chapter 3.
Triads: Strings ③②① ④③② ⑤④③ ⑥⑤④

Major

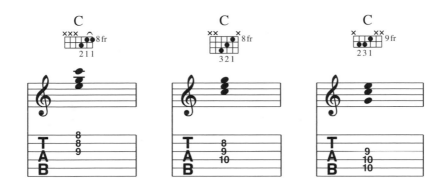

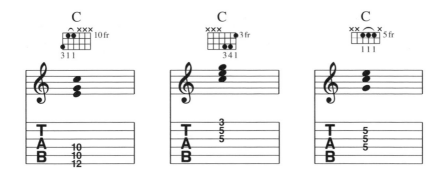

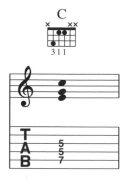

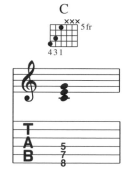

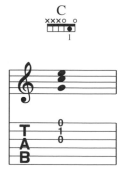

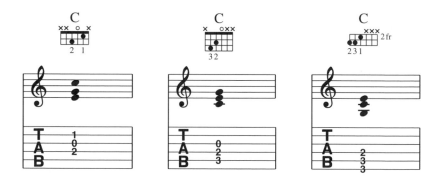

Minor

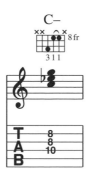

Suspended 4

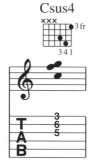

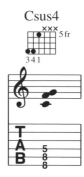

Diminished

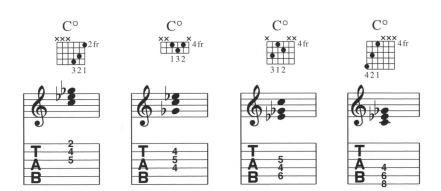

TRIADS: STRINGS ③②① ④③② ⑤④③ ⑥⑤④

Augmented

18

Open Triadic Shapes: Major across String Sets

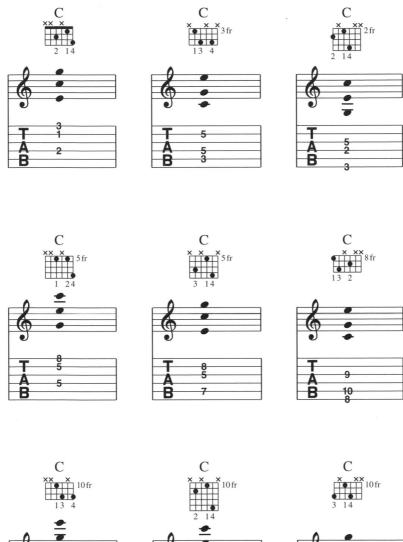

Open Triadic Shapes: Minor across String Sets

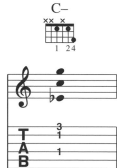

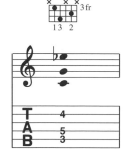

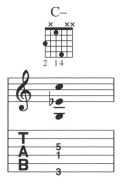

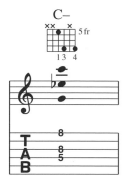

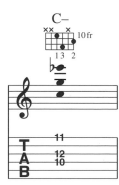

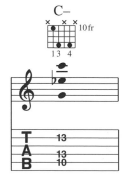

Chapter 4.
Barre Chords with Roots on ⑥ and ⑤

Sixth String Root Names for Barre Chords with Bass Notes on 6th String

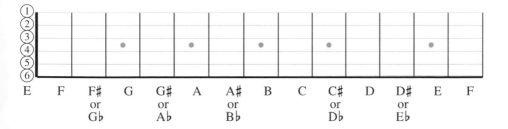

E	F	F# or Gb	G	G# or Ab	A	A# or Bb	B	C	C# or Db	D	D# or Eb	E	F

Fifth String Root Names for Barre Chords with Bass Notes on 5th String

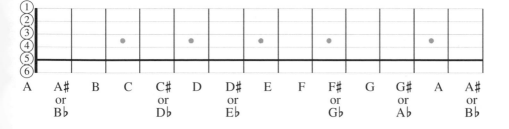

A	A# or Bb	B	C	C# or Db	D	D# or Eb	E	F	F# or Gb	G	G# or Ab	A	A# or Bb

Major

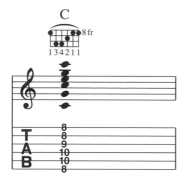 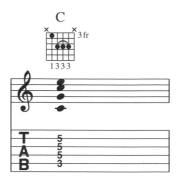

Minor

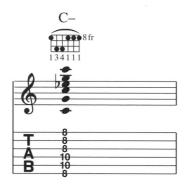 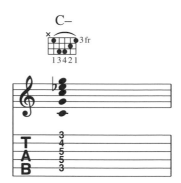

Suspended 4

 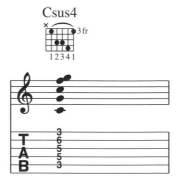

Minor 7

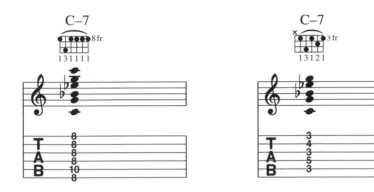

Dominant 7

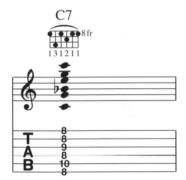

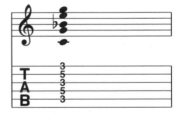

Dominant 7(9)

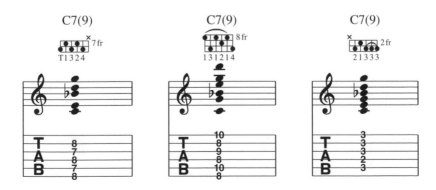

Diminished 7

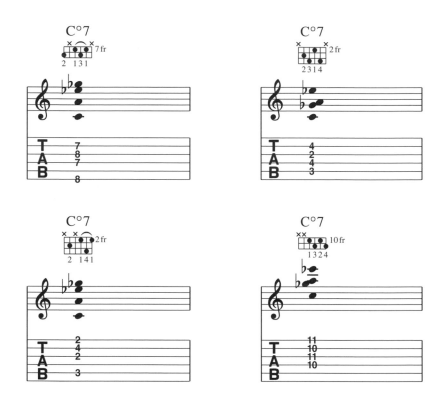

Augmented 7 (Dominant 7♯5)

Note: These are the same notes as C7(♭13). A♭ is the enharmonic equivalent of G♯.

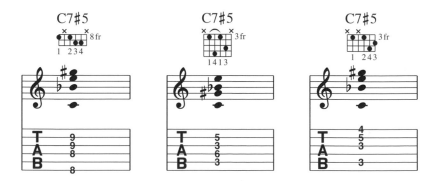

Chapter 5.
Other Common Voicings

Dominant 7(9)

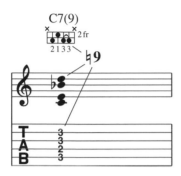

Dominant 7(♯9)

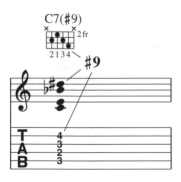

Dominant 7(♭9)

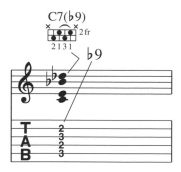

Dominant 7sus4

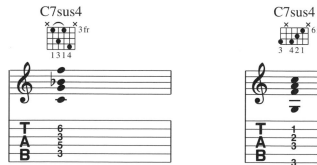

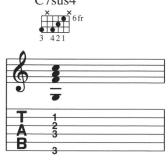

Chapter 6.
Using Open Tunings

Tune the low E string down to D to play the chords in this chapter.

Drop D

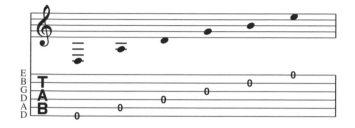

D Major   **D Major add9**

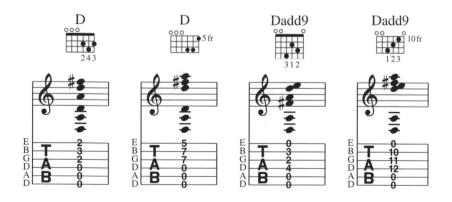

D Major 9

D Minor

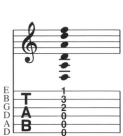

D Minor add9

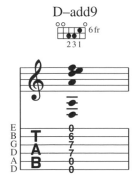

D Minor 9

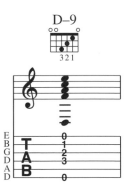

E Major

E Minor

F Major

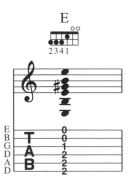

F Major 7

F Minor

E♭ Major 9

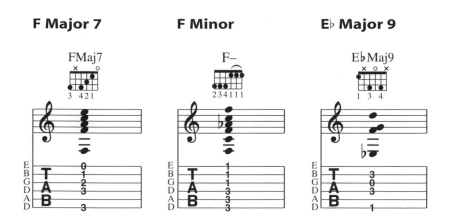

Double-Drop D

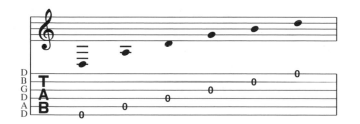

C add9

A Major add4

A Minor (11)

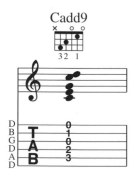

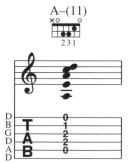

G Major

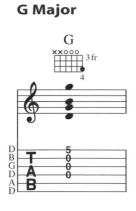

E Major

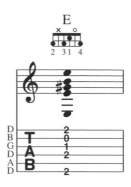

E Minor

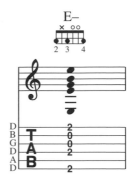

D Major

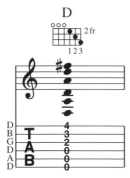

D add9

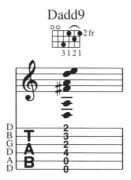

C Major

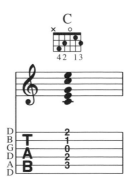

C Major add9   A Major add4

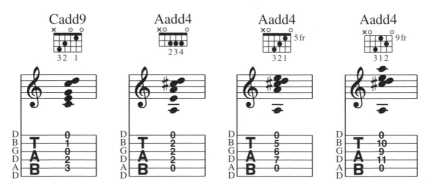

D Major   D Major add9   D Dominant 7

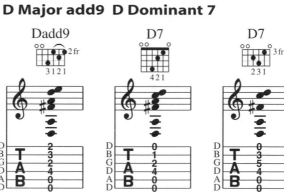
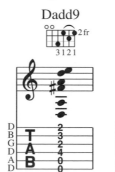

D Dominant 7(9)   D Dominant 7(13)

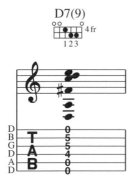
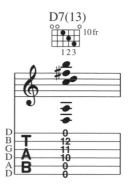

G Major   G Dominant 7

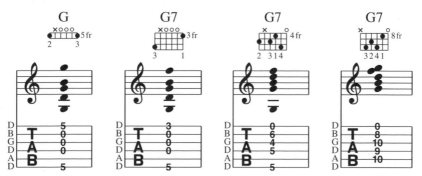

E♭ Major (9)

E♭ Minor

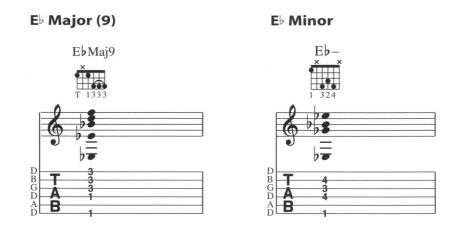

Open G Tuning: DGDGBD

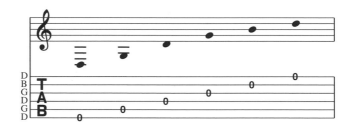

G Major

C Major add9 over G

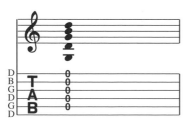

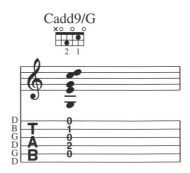

C Dominant 7

C 7(9)

C Major

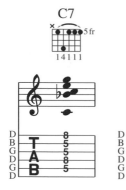

A Minor over G

A Minor

A Minor (11)

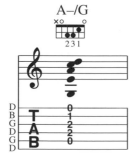
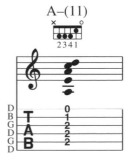

G Major

G Dominant 7

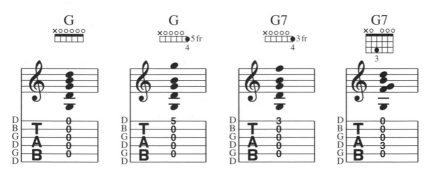

G Dominant 7(9)

G7(9)

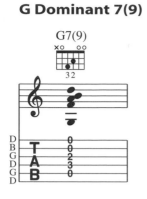

E Major

E

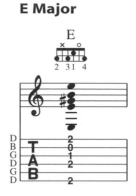

E Dominant 7

E7

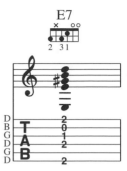

E Minor

E–

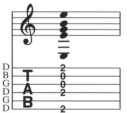

E Minor 7

E–7

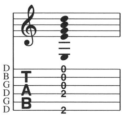

D Dominant 7

D7

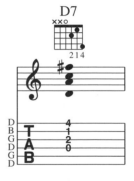

D Dominant 7(9)

D7(9)

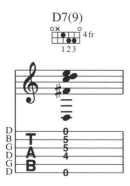

E♭ Major 7

E♭Maj7

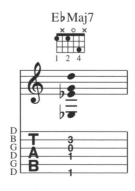

E♭ Major 9

E♭Maj9

Etude: Triads through Cycle 4 in Open G Tuning

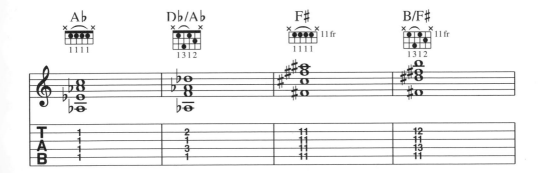

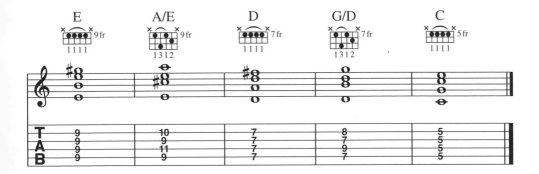

PART II.
GLOSSARY OF COMMON CHORD VOICINGS

Key of C

Major

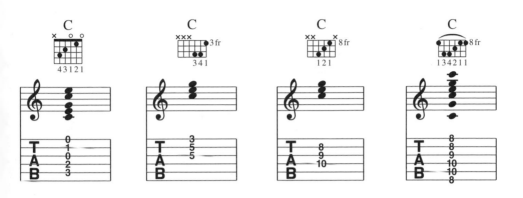

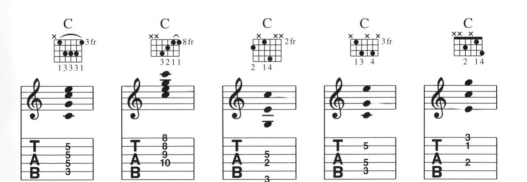

Minor

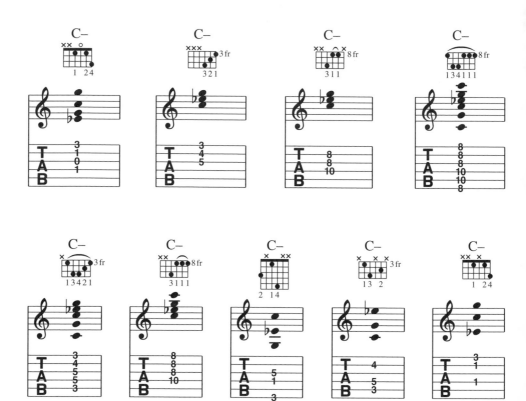

Sus4

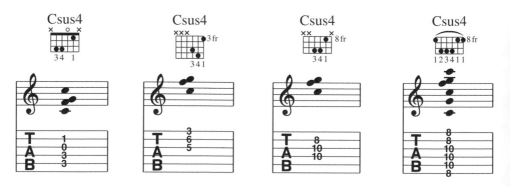

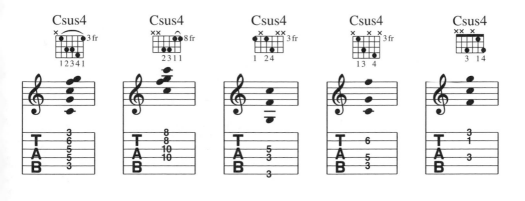

Diminished

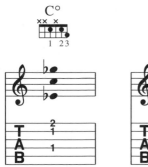
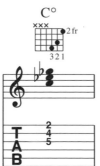
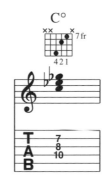

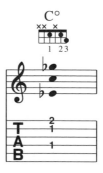

Augmented

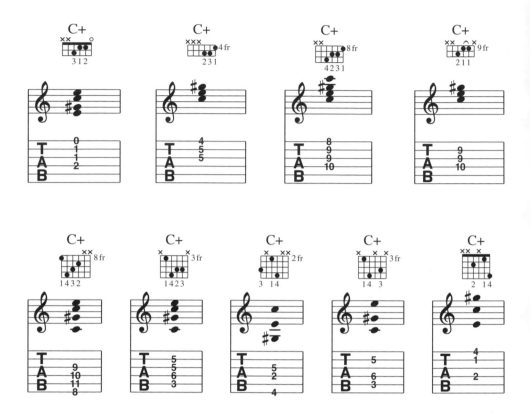

Dominant 7

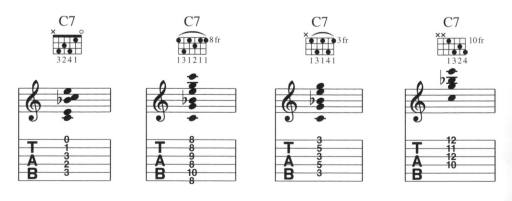

Dominant 7(9)

Dominant 7(♯9)

Dominant 7(♭9)

Dominant 7♯5

Dominant 7sus4

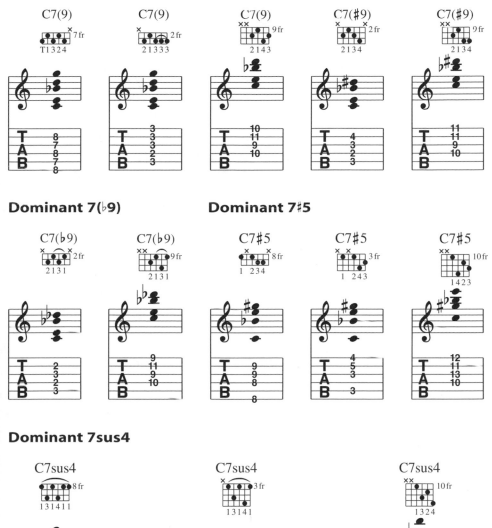

Major 7

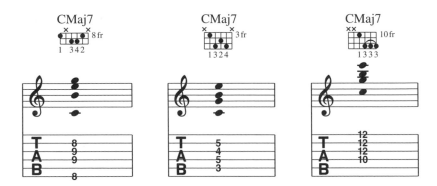

Minor 7

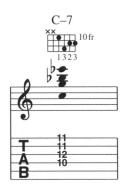

Diminished 7

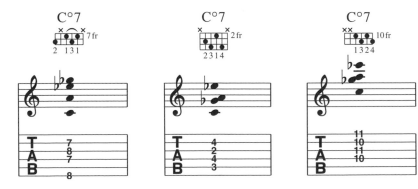

Key of D♭

Major

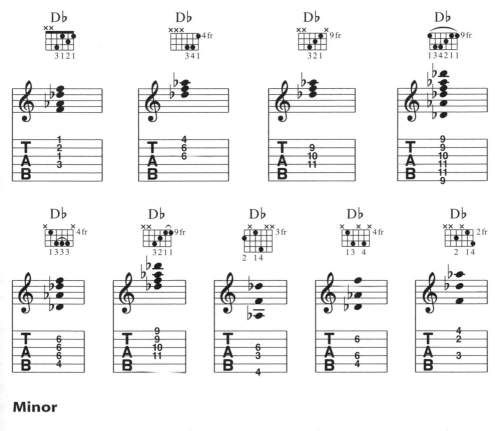

Minor

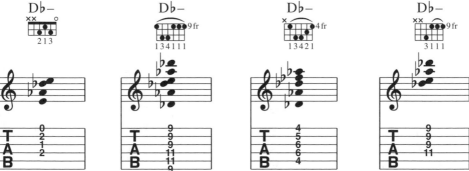

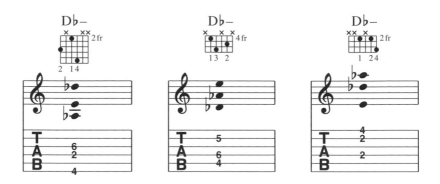

Sus4

  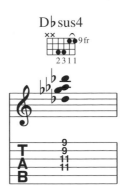

 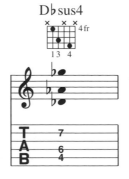 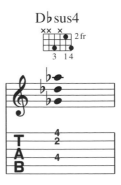

Diminished

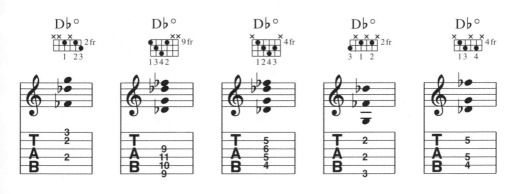

Augmented

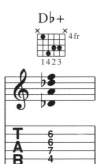

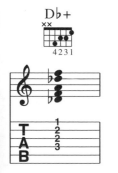

Dominant 7

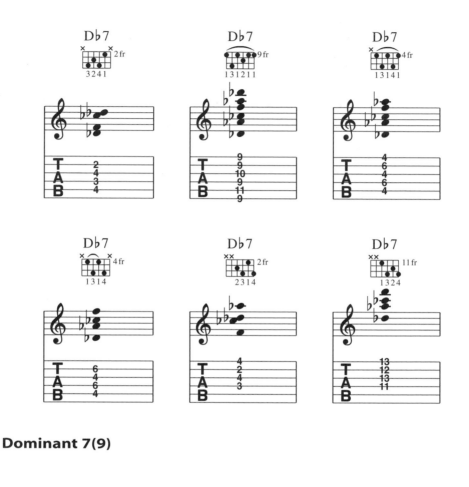

Dominant 7(9)

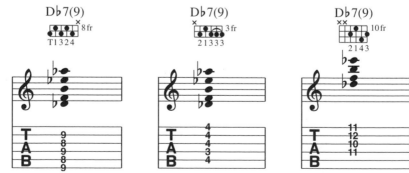

Dominant 7(#9)

Dominant 7(♭9)

Dominant 7#5

Dominant 7sus4

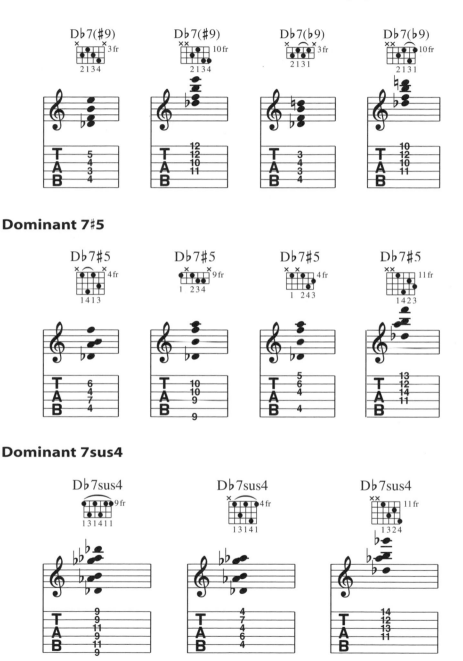

Major 7

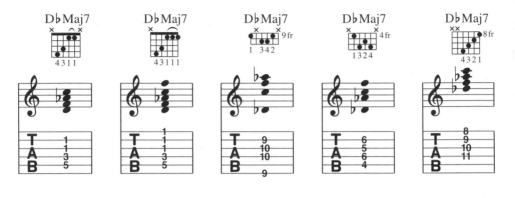

Minor 7

Diminished 7

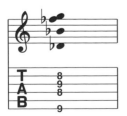
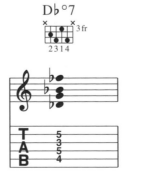
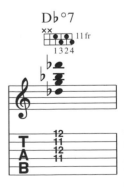

Key of D

Major

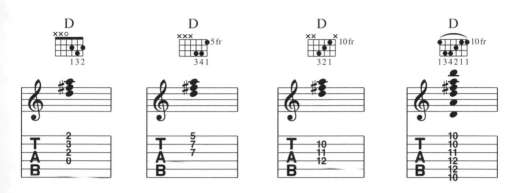

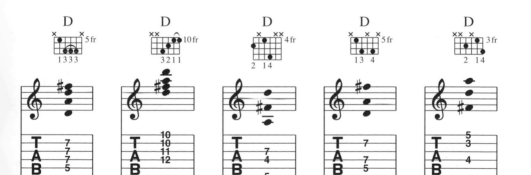

Minor

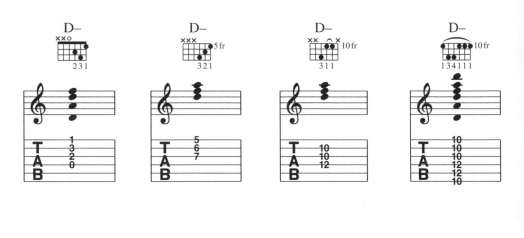

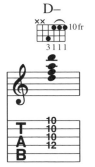
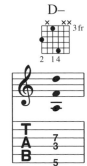

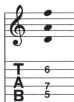

Sus4

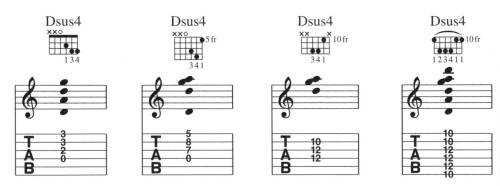

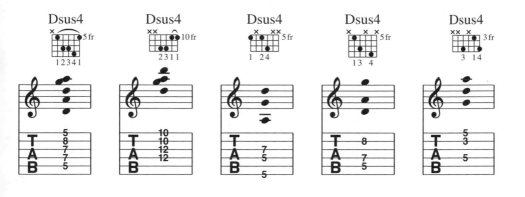

Diminished

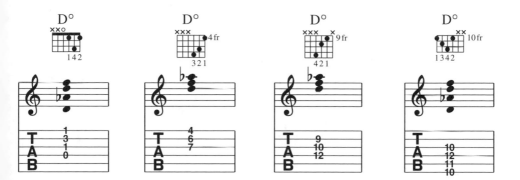

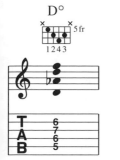
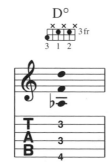

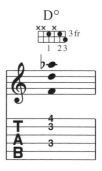

Augmented

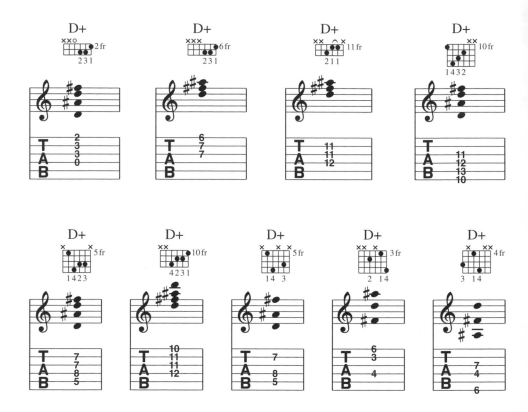

Dominant 7

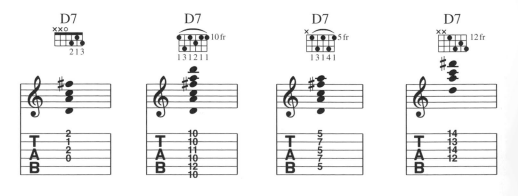

Dominant 7(9)

Dominant 7(♯9)

Dominant 7(♭9)

Dominant 7♯5

Dominant 7sus4

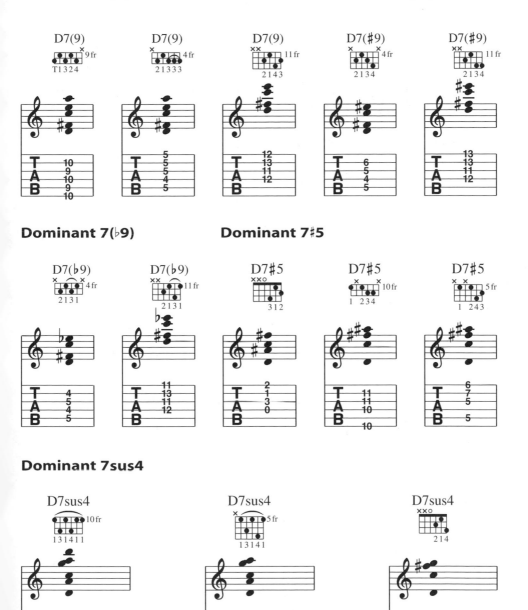

Major 7

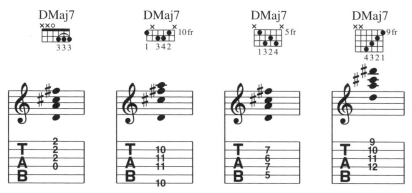

Minor 7

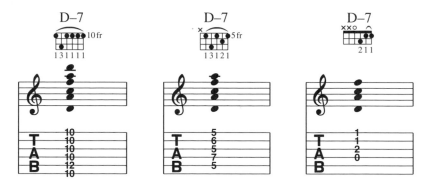

Diminished 7

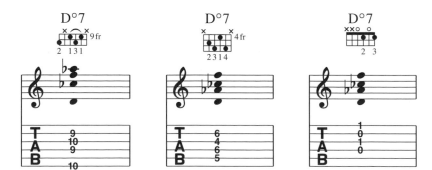

Key of E♭

Major

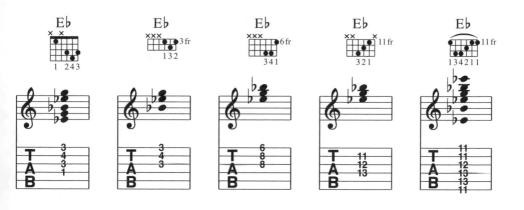

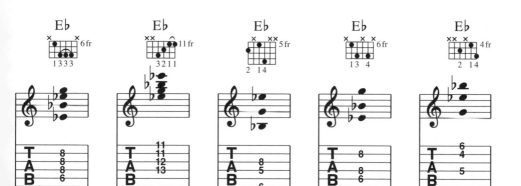

Minor

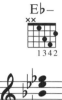

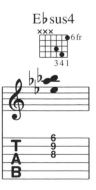

Sus4

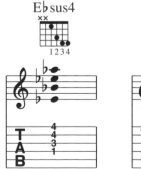

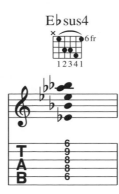

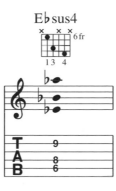

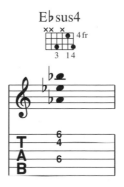

Diminished

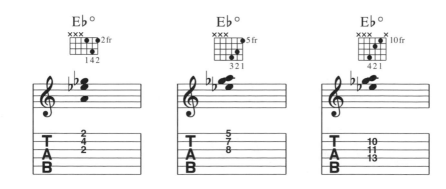

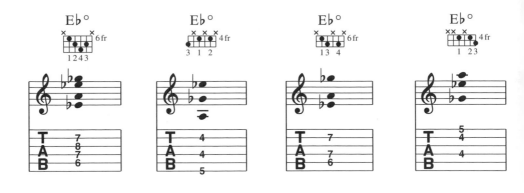

Augmented

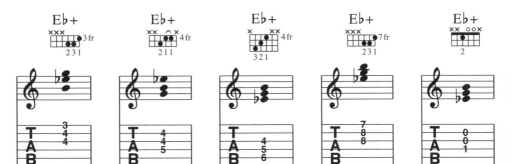

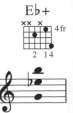

Dominant 7

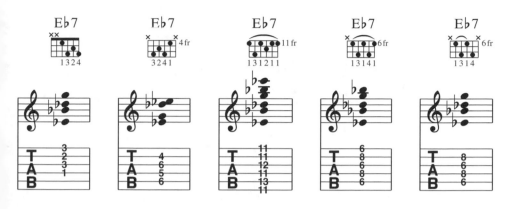

Dominant 7(9)

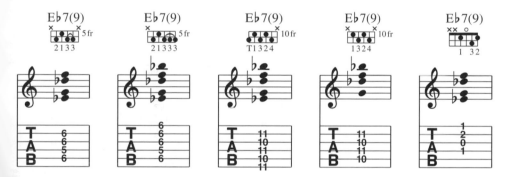

Dominant 7(♯9)

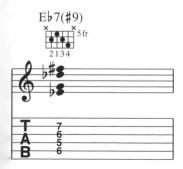

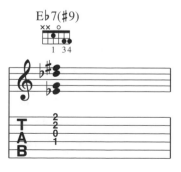

Dominant 7(♭9)

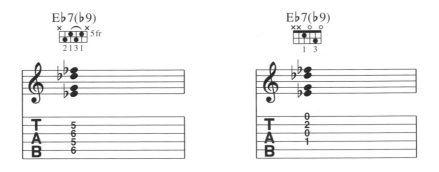

Dominant 7#5

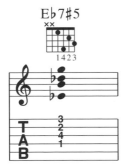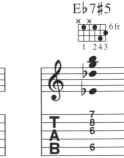

Dominant 7sus4

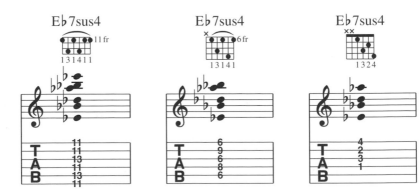

Major 7

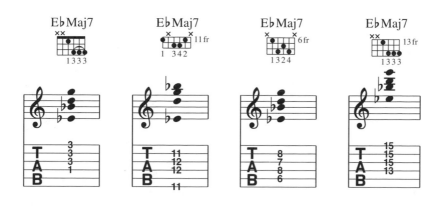

Eb Maj7   Eb Maj7   Eb Maj7   Eb Maj7

Minor 7

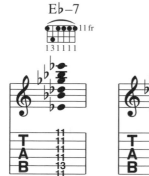

Eb−7   Eb−7   Eb−7   Eb−7

Diminished 7

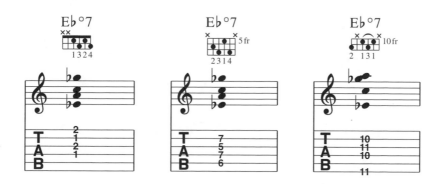

Eb°7   Eb°7   Eb°7

Key of E

Major

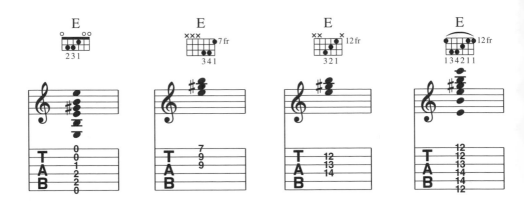

Minor

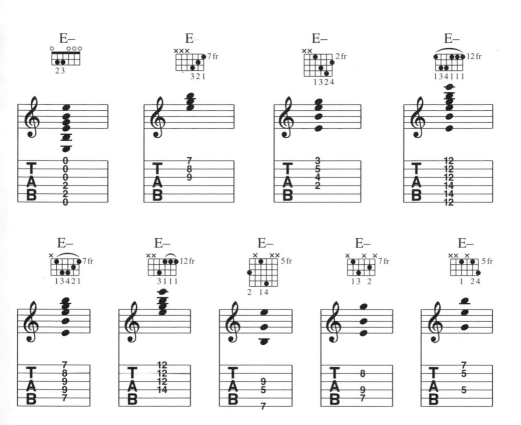

Sus4

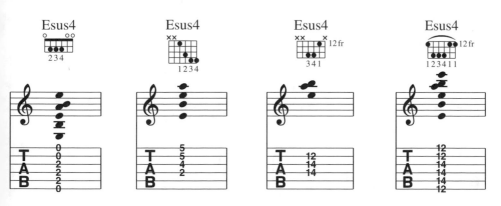

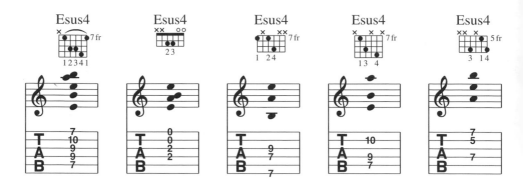

Diminished

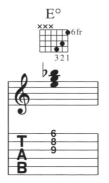
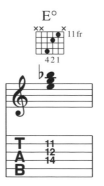

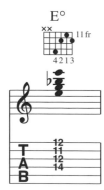

Augmented

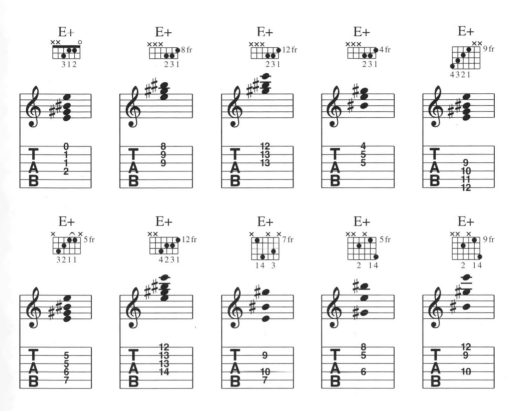

Dominant 7

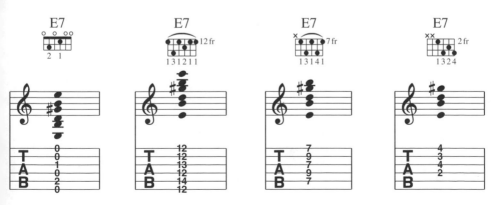

Dominant 7(9)

Dominant 7(♯9)

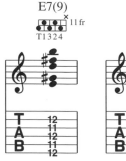

Dominant 7(♭9)

Dominant 7♯5

Dominant 7sus4

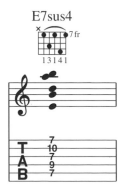

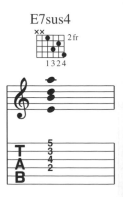

Major 7

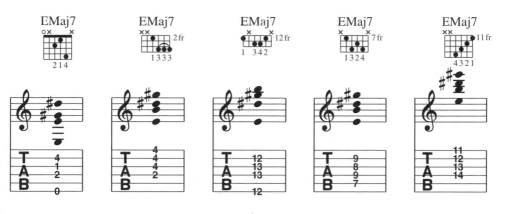

Minor 7

Diminished 7

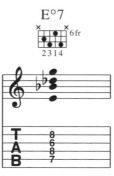

Key of F

Major

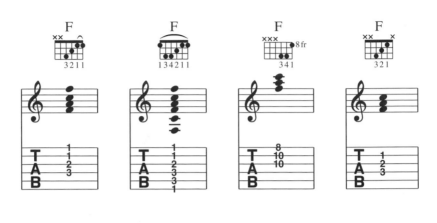

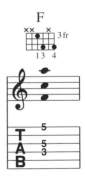

Minor

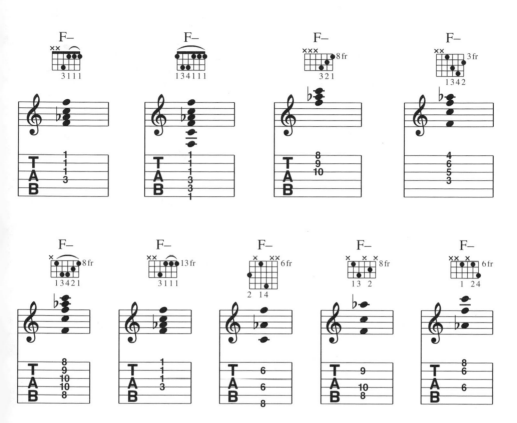

Sus4

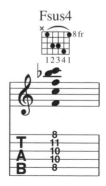

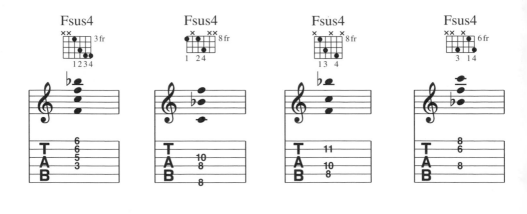

Diminished

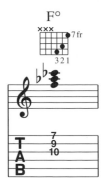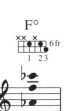

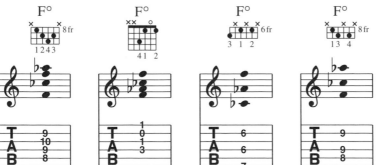

Augmented

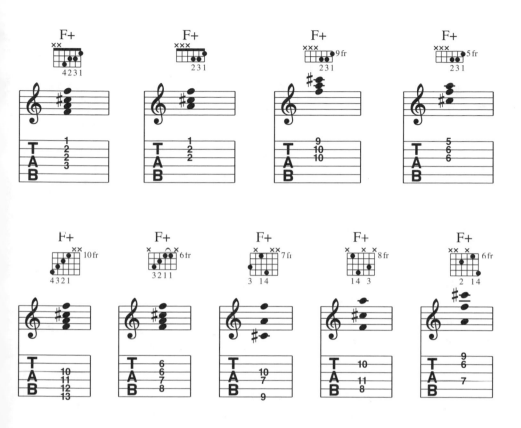

Dominant 7

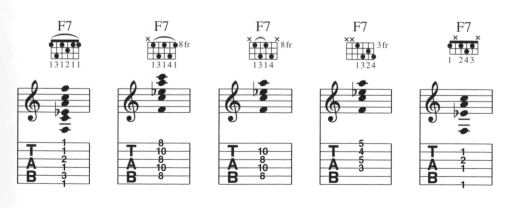

Dominant 7(9)

Dominant 7(♯9)

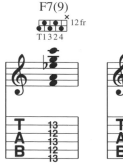

F7(9)

F7(9)

F7(9)

F7(♯9)

F7(♯9)

Dominant 7(♭9)

Dominant 7♯5

F7(♭9)

F7(♭9)

F7♯5

F7♯5

F7♯5

Dominant 7sus4

F7sus4

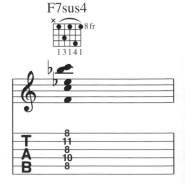

F7sus4

Major 7

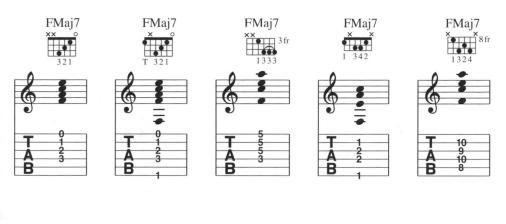

FMaj7   FMaj7   FMaj7   FMaj7   FMaj7

F–7   F–7   F–7   F–7

Minor 7

F°7   F°7   F°7

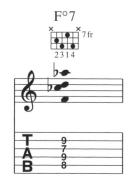

Key of F♯

Major

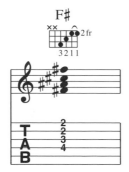

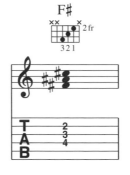

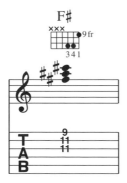

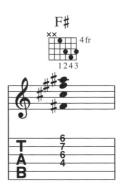

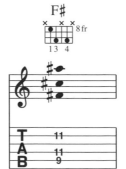

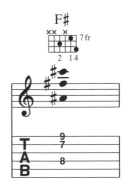

Minor

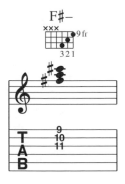

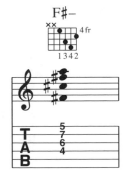

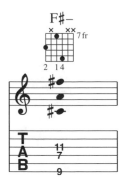

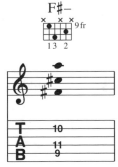

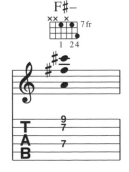

Sus4

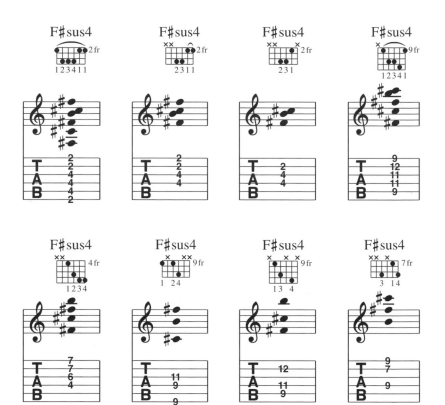

Diminished

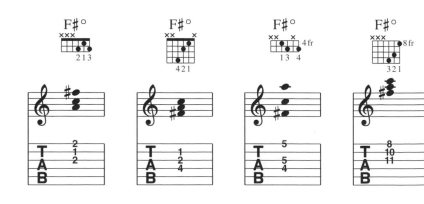

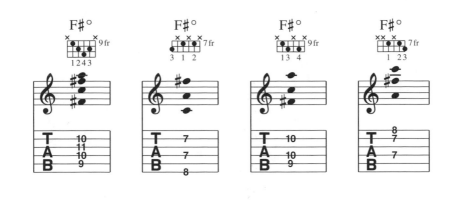

Augmented

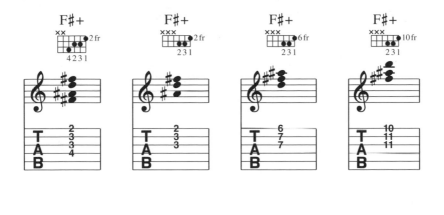

Dominant 7

Dominant 7(9)

Dominant 7(#9)

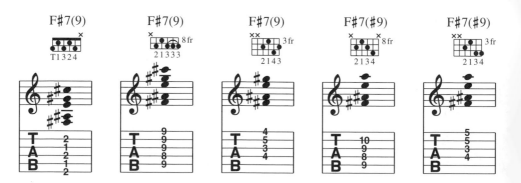

Dominant 7(♭9)

Dominant 7♯5

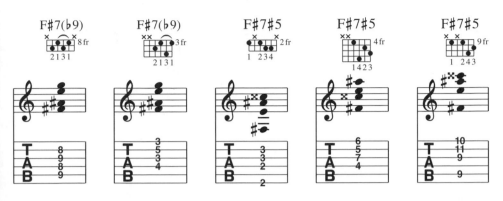

Dominant 7sus4

Major 7

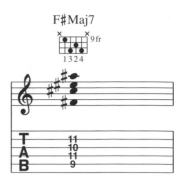

Minor 7

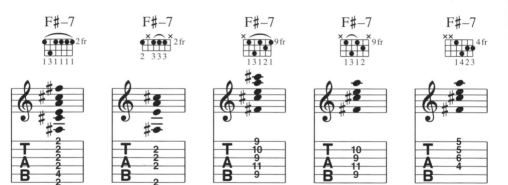

Diminished 7

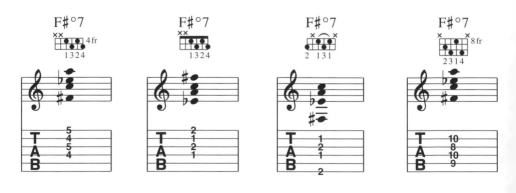

Key of G

Major

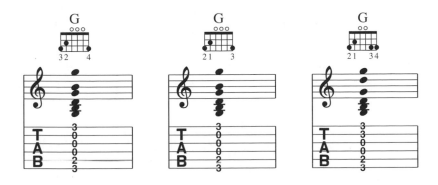

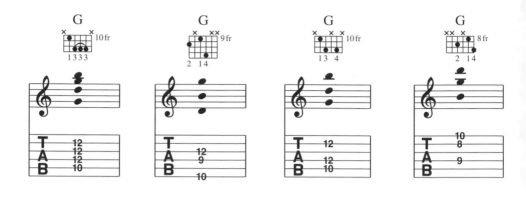

Minor

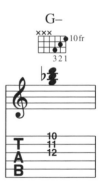

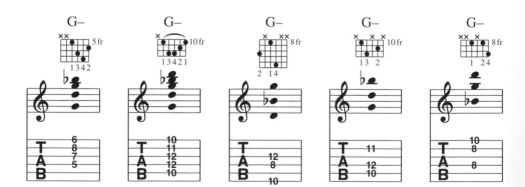

Sus4

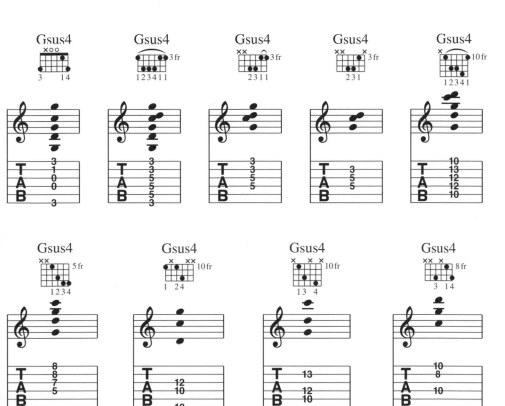

Diminished

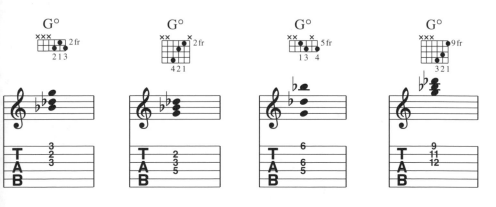

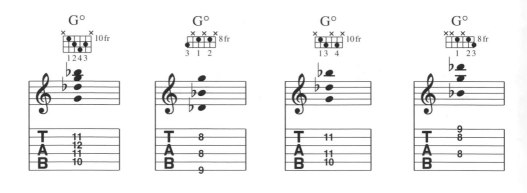

Augmented

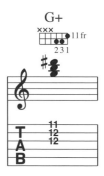

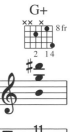

Dominant 7

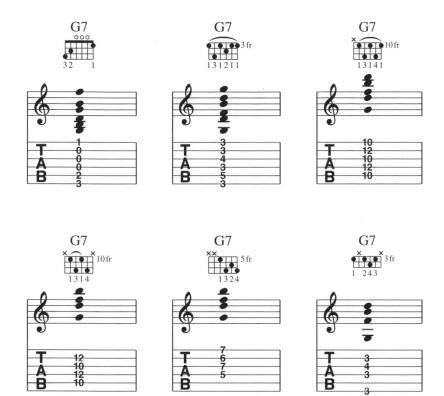

Dominant 7(9)

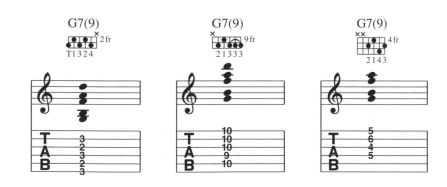

Dominant 7(#9)

Dominant 7(♭9)

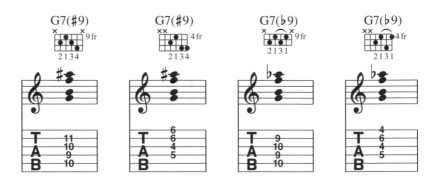

Dominant 7#5

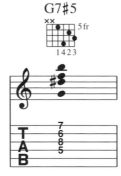

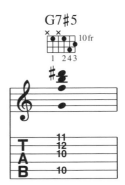

Dominant 7sus4

Major 7

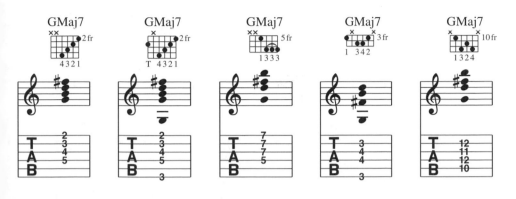

Minor 7

Diminished 7

  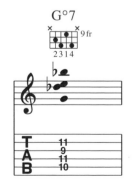

Key of A♭

Major

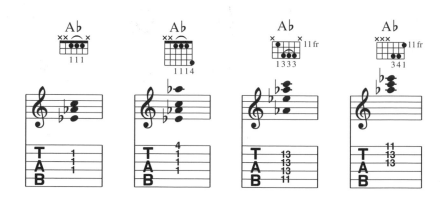

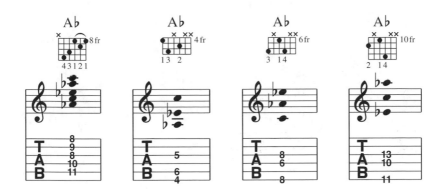

Minor

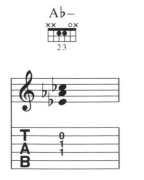

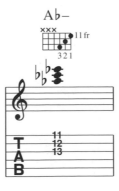
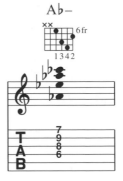

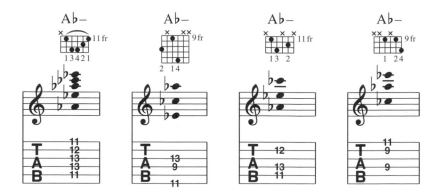

Sus4

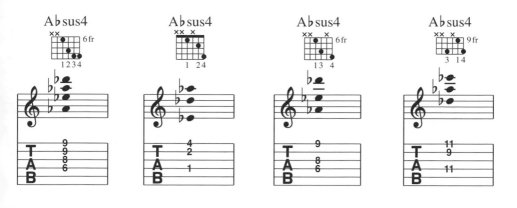

Diminished

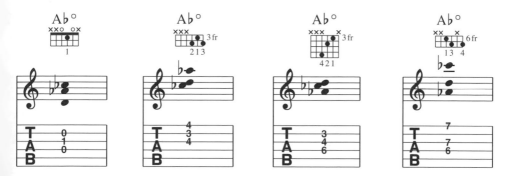

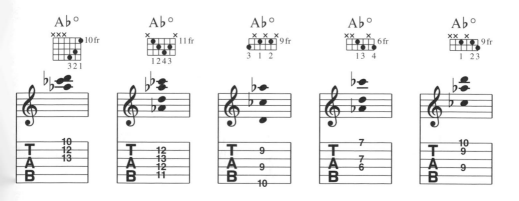

Augmented

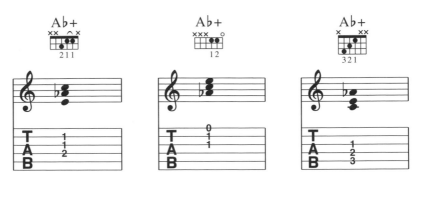

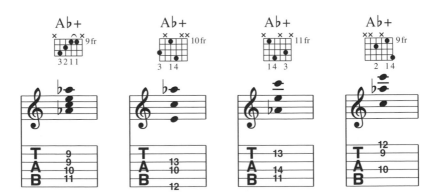

Dominant 7

Dominant 7(9)

 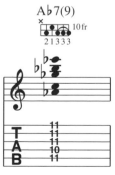 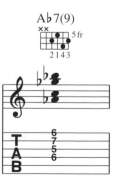

Dominant 7(#9)

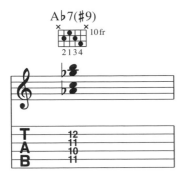

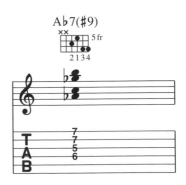

Dominant 7(♭9)

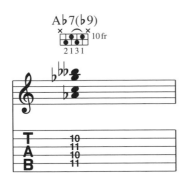

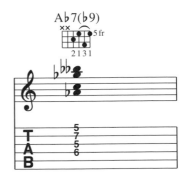

Dominant 7#5

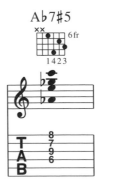

Dominant 7sus4

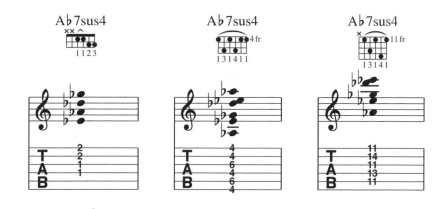

Ab7sus4   Ab7sus4   Ab7sus4

Major 7

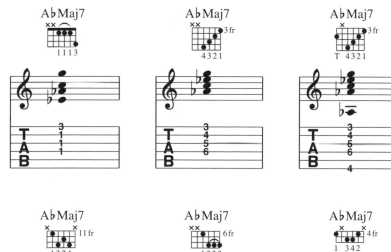

AbMaj7   AbMaj7   AbMaj7

AbMaj7   AbMaj7   AbMaj7

Minor 7

Diminished 7

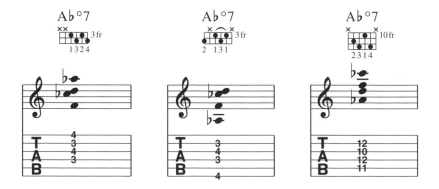

Key of A

Major

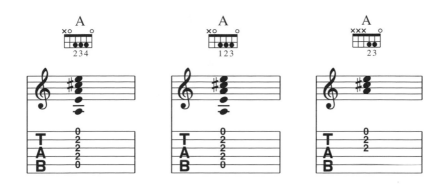

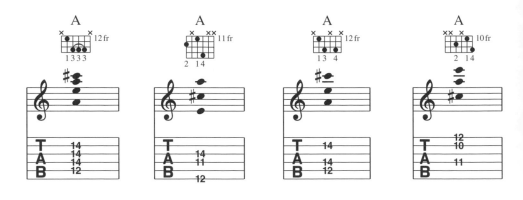

Minor

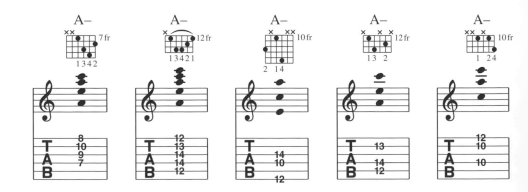

Sus4

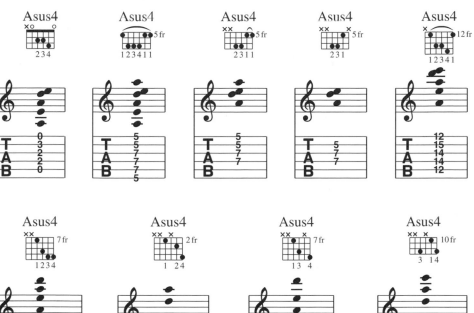

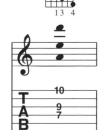

Diminished

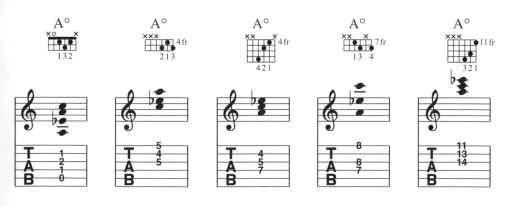

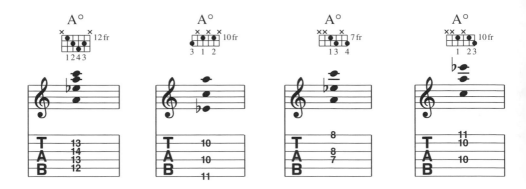

Augmented

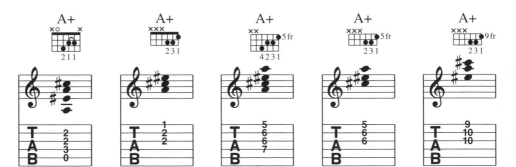

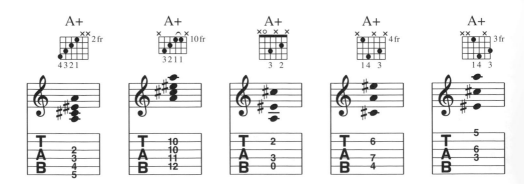

Dominant 7

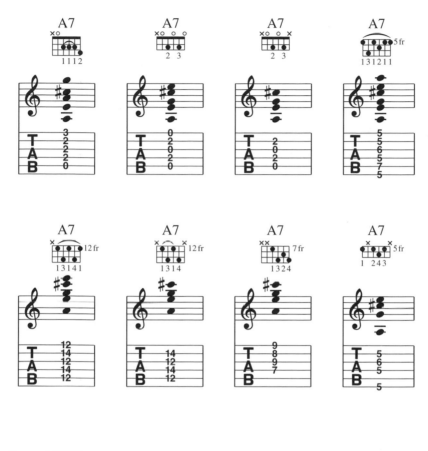

Dominant 7(9)

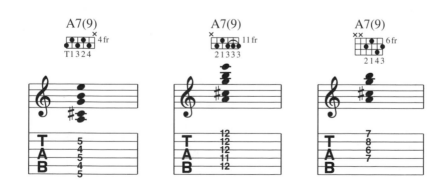

Dominant 7(#9)

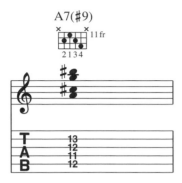

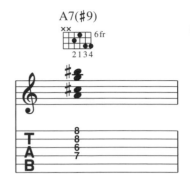

Dominant 7(♭9)

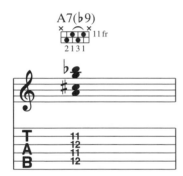

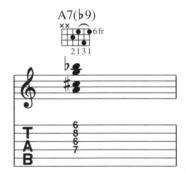

Dominant 7#5

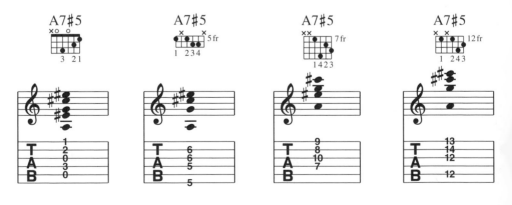

Dominant 7sus4

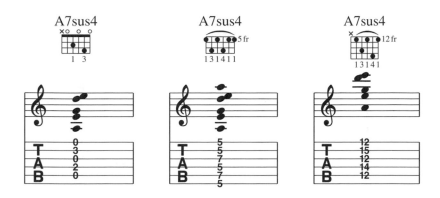

Major 7

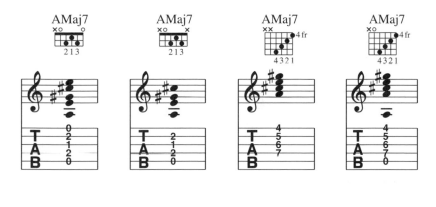

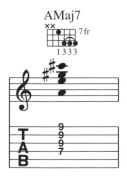

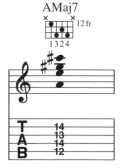

Minor 7

Diminished 7

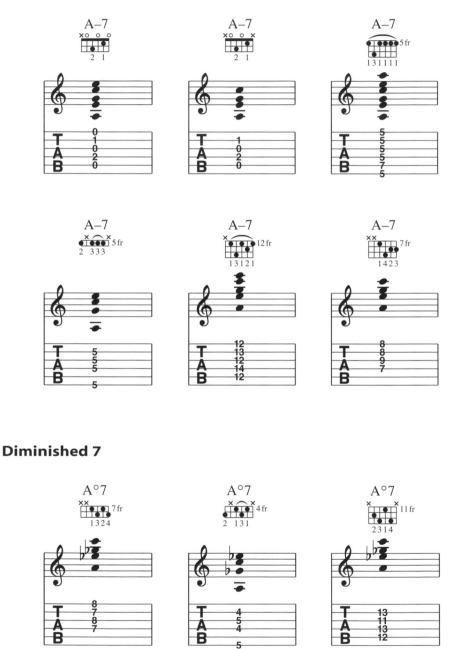

Key of B♭

Major

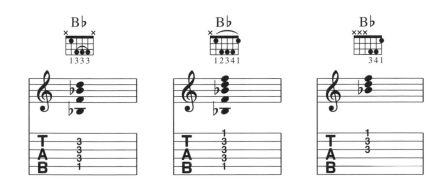

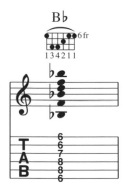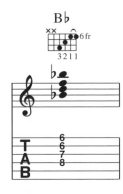

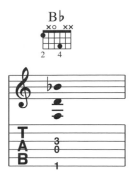
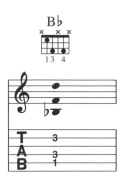
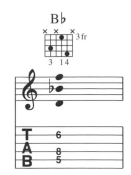

Minor

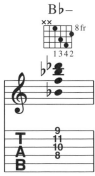

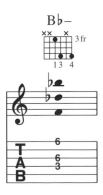

Sus4

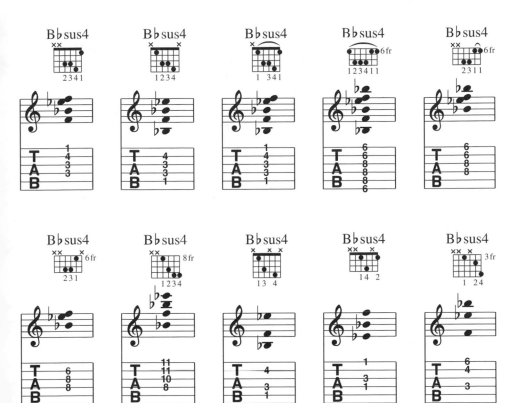

Diminished

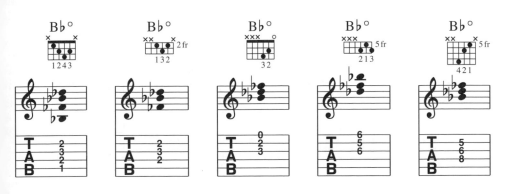

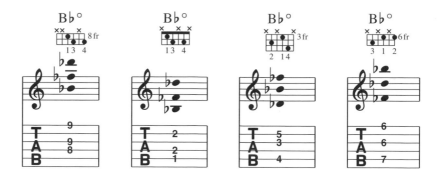

Augmented

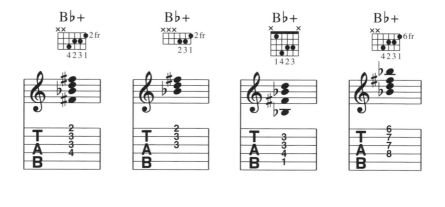

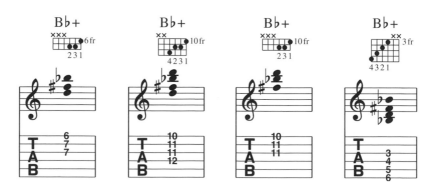

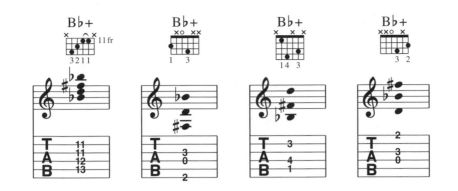

Dominant 7

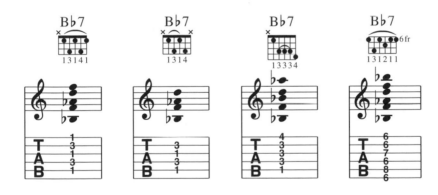

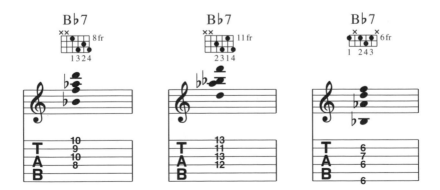

Dominant 7(9)

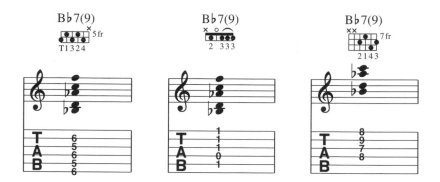

Dominant 7(♯9)

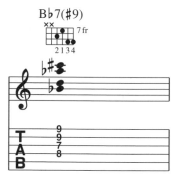

Dominant 7(♭9)

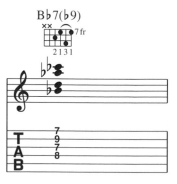

Dominant 7#5

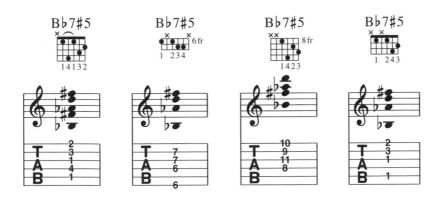

Dominant 7sus4

Major 7

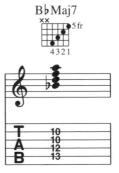

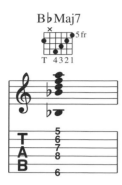
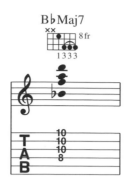

Minor 7

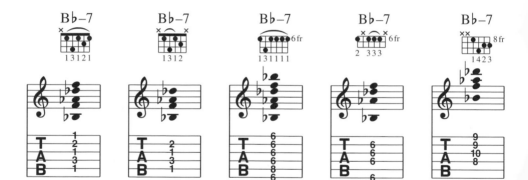

Diminished 7

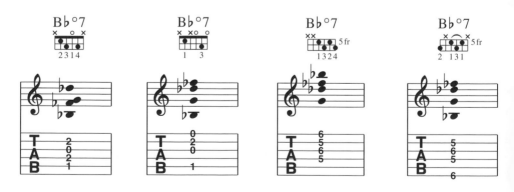

Key of B

Major

Minor

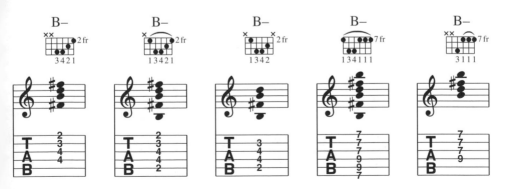

113

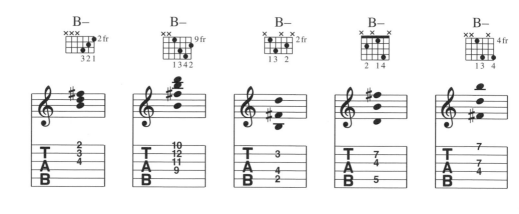

Sus4

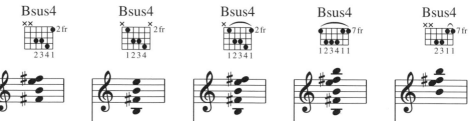

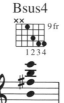

Diminished

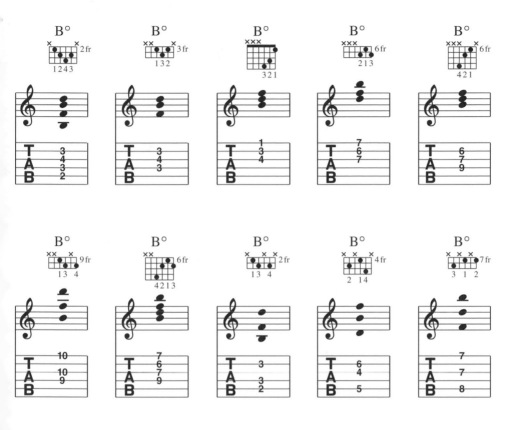

Augmented

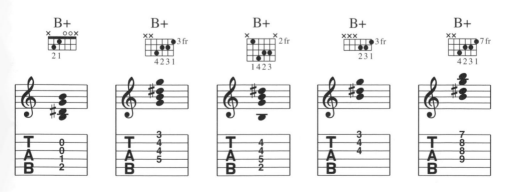

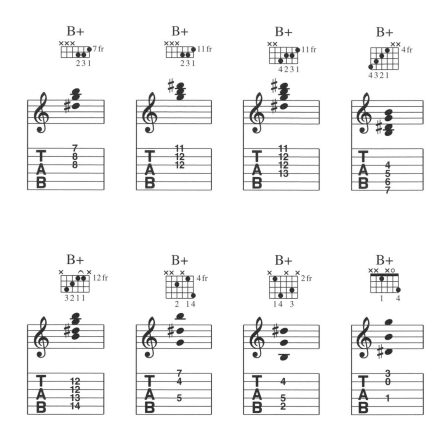

Dominant 7

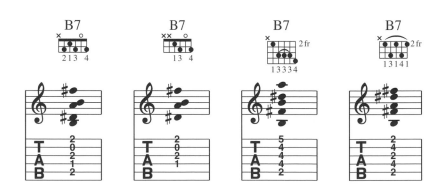

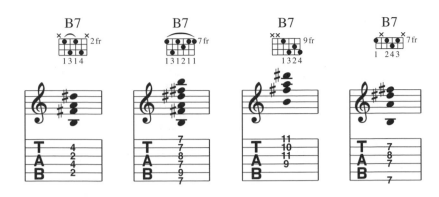

Dominant 7(9)

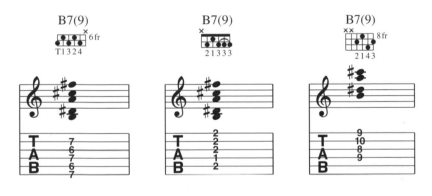

Dominant 7(#9)   ## Dominant 7(♭9)

Dominant 7♯5

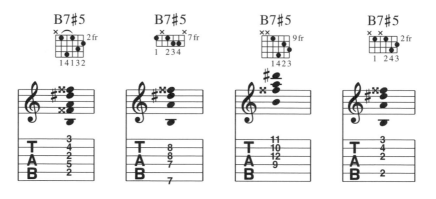

Dominant 7sus4

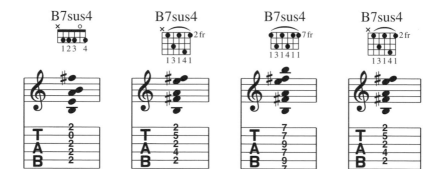

Major 7

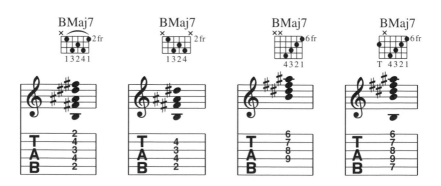

BMaj7

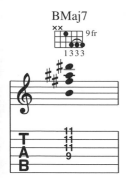

Minor 7

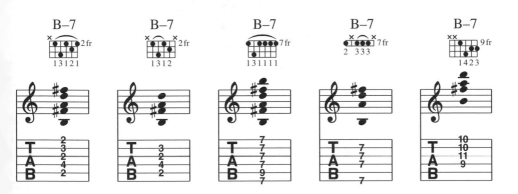

Diminished 7

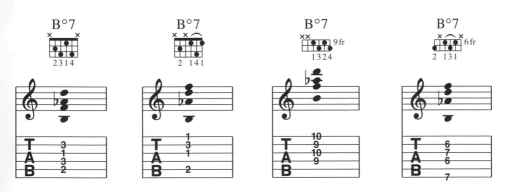

About the Author

Photo by Craig Reed

Rick Peckham is an internationally known jazz guitarist, clinician, composer, and writer. In addition to extensive work in the U.S., he has led or played on tours of Ireland, Canada, Spain, and Germany. His trio recording *Left End*, with drummer Jim Black and bassist Tony Scherr, was named one of the best releases of 2005 by *DownBeat* magazine. Peckham has been a Berklee faculty member since 1986, serving as Assistant Chair of the Guitar Department, with 1100 guitar students and sixty guitar faculty, since 1992. He organized the college's honorary doctoral tributes to Roy Haynes, Joe Zawinul, Jack DeJohnette, and John Scofield, featuring then-Berklee students Kurt Rosenwinkel, Matthew Garrison, Antonio Hart, Abe Laboriel Jr., Melvin Butler, and Seamus Blake. His other Berklee Media works include the DVD *Modal Voicing Techniques*, the book *The Berklee Jazz Guitar Chord Dictionary*, and two 12-week online courses: Berklee Guitar Chords 101 (2007 UCEA award for best online class) and Berklee Guitar Chords 201 on Berkleemusic.com.

For further information regarding upcoming performances and projects, please see www.rickpeckham.com.